The Book of Chocolate

The Book of Chocolate

Patricia Lousada

EBURY
PRESS

Published by Ebury Press
National Magazine House
72 Broadwick Street
London W 1 V 2BP

First impression 1984

© Patricia Lousada 1984
© Illustrations E T Archive Ltd 1984

Edited, designed and illustrated by
the E T Archive Ltd, Chelsea Wharf,
15 Lots Road, London SW 10 0QH

Designer Julian Holland
Photography Eileen Tweedy

ISBN 0 85223 378 7

Phototypeset in Great Britain by
Tradespools Limited, Frome, Somerset
Printed and bound by New Interlitho s.p.a., Milan

Contents

Introduction

Chocolate came to Europe in the sixteenth century. It was introduced to the Spanish court by the explorer Cortéz, who first drank it at the court of Montezuma. The Spaniards sweetened the bitter Mexican drink and managed to guard the secret of its cultivation and preparation for nearly one hundred years. By the seventeenth century the secret was out and chocolate houses serving the drink were popular meeting-places for the well-to-do throughout Europe. By the early eighteenth century chocolate was commerically manufactured. Prices dropped and chocolate became increasingly popular. But it was not until a century later that eating chocolate was born. The Dutchman Coenraad J van Houten invented a press to extract cocoa butter from the bean and paved the way twenty years later for the Englishman, Joseph Fry, to produce the first eating chocolate.

Today chocolate is more the rage than ever. Ice creams and icings, soufflés and sauces, cookies and cakes are at their most popular when rich and dark in chocolate.

This book contains chocolate treats for all occasions. I have included some rich but light chocolate desserts that are elegant as well as delicious. The Chocolate chestnut mousse cake and the Mousse suprême au framboise are desserts for dinner parties that can be prepared ahead of time and look enticing on the plate.

I am grateful and very fortunate to be able to include three fabulous chocolate creations from three famous cooks: Katie Stewart's unbeatable Chocolate roulade; Marquise au chocolat blanc from Brian Turner of London's Capital Hotel; and the delectable Tarte au chocolat from French chef Christian Germain of the Château Montreuil. All three are perfect party pieces.

Sainsbury's has kindly given permission to reprint Brownies and Chocolate Chip Cookies from my *American Sampler*.

Hints for cooking with chocolate

Use only the best plain eating chocolate. Look for brands containing a minimum of 50% cocoa solids. When cocoa powder is called for, use only a pure one with no additives.

White chocolate is made with cocoa butter, milk and sugar. It does not contain chocolate liquor and does not have a real chocolate flavour.

Use vanilla extract and not vanilla flavouring which is synthetic. If it is difficult to obtain, replace the sugar with vanilla sugar in any recipe calling for vanilla extract. This can be made by storing 2–3 vanilla pods with caster sugar.

Have all your ingredients at the same temperature for smooth blending and fold them in with a large metal spoon, incorporating as much air as possible.

A copper bowl for whisking egg whites ensures the maximum volume. The bowl and whisk you use should be well washed; add a squeeze of lemon or vinegar before the final rinse.

Hints for melting chocolate

Break the chocolate into small pieces so that it can melt evenly.

Never melt chocolate over direct heat. The flavour will be impaired and it will 'sieze' (go hard and grainy) if it becomes too hot.

To melt chocolate—boil a small amount of water in the bottom of a double saucepan. The bottom of the top pan should not touch the water, and should fit tightly to avoid steam coming in contact with the chocolate. Take the pan off the heat, and add the chocolate. Cover and leave until the chocolate has melted.

Chocolate can be melted with a small amount of liquid (not less than 1 tbsp). But if a small amount of liquid is added after the chocolate has melted it will 'sieze'. If this should happen, you may be able to retrieve it by adding a little oil.

Chocolate may be safely added to a large quantity of hot liquid. Butter or oil can be added before or after chocolate has melted without any risk.

Measures
1 teaspoon (tsp) = 5 ml
1 tablespoon (tbsp) = 15 ml

Chocolate Artichoke

1 globe artichoke
450 g (1 lb) plain chocolate in small pieces
2 tbsp sunflower or groundnut oil
4–5 drops peppermint oil (optional)

To assemble the artichoke
small piece of cake
25 g (1 oz) caster sugar
25 g (1 oz) butter
2 tbsp water
50 g (2 oz) icing sugar
25 g (1 oz) cocoa powder

An amusing finale for a special occasion. The leaves can be pulled off and eaten as an after dinner mint.

Boil a small amount of water in the bottom of a double saucepan. The bottom of the top pan should not touch the water and should fit tightly to avoid steam coming in contact with the chocolate. Take the pan off the heat and add the chocolate and oil, cover

the pan and leave, stirring occasionally, until the chocolate has melted. The chocolate should not exceed a temperature of 55°C/110°F. Allow the chocolate to drop to a temperature of 45°C/90–95°F before dipping. Stir in the oil of peppermint. Peel the leaves off the artichoke and dip the front side of the leaves in the chocolate. Lay out on a surface covered with non-stick baking parchment. Leave overnight before peeling away the artichoke leaves. Dissolve the caster sugar in the butter and water over low heat. Off the heat stir in the sieved icing sugar and cocoa powder. Cut a 6 cm (2½ in) diameter base, pyramid-shaped cake and cover with the icing. Stick the chocolate leaves around the cake in the same order as the real artichoke. Use extra frosting to help make them stick.

For a white artichoke replace the plain chocolate with white and omit the oil, oil of peppermint and cocoa powder.

Chocolate Raspberry Meringue

To serve 10

4 egg whites
pinch of salt
250 g (9 oz) caster sugar
25 g (1 oz) cocoa powder
100 g (4 oz) hazelnuts, shelled and ground
1 tsp of vanilla extract
450 g (1 lb) raspberries, fresh or frozen
300 ml ($\frac{1}{2}$ pint) double cream

Grease and line the bottom of two 20 cm (8 in) sandwich tins with non-stick baking parchment. Preheat oven to 190° C/375° F/ mark 5. Whisk the egg whites with the salt until stiff, add the sugar a little at a time and continue to whisk until the mixture is very stiff. Sift the cocoa over the mixture and fold in, then fold in the vanilla extract and the ground nuts. Divide the mixture between the tins and smooth the tops with a palette knife. Bake for 30–35 minutes— the tops will be crisp but the insides still soft. Leave in the tins for 10 minutes before turning out onto a rack to cool. The meringues can be made a few days ahead if kept in an airtight container. Whip the cream, sandwich the meringues with half the cream and raspberries and use the remaining cream and raspberries for the top. Prepare 3 hours before serving so cake can be cut without splintering.

Tarte Au Chocolat

To serve 8–10

For the cake
45 g (scant 2 oz) cake flour
150 g (5 oz) caster sugar
3 large eggs
75 g (3 oz) plain chocolate
25 g (1 oz) cocoa
100 g (4 oz) unsalted butter

For the kumquats
450 g (1 lb) kumquats
300 ml (½ pint) water
150 g (5 oz) sugar

For the glaze
100 g (4 oz) plain chocolate
25 g (1 oz) unsalted butter
2 tbsp milk

Grease a 20 cm (8 in) shallow round cake tin and line with non-stick parchment paper. With an electric whisk, beat the flour, sugar and eggs for about 10 minutes, or until they are very thick and can leave a ribbon trail when the whisk is lifted. Meanwhile melt the chocolate, cocoa and butter in a double saucepan over barely simmering water. Add this to the egg mixture and continue to whisk for another 8 minutes. Pour into the tin and bake in a preheated oven 150°C/300°F/mark 2 for 25 minutes. Remove and rest in the tin for 10 minutes. Turn out onto a cake rack and pour over the melted glaze. Allow the glaze to set but serve while still lukewarm with the kumquats spooned over each slice.

For the kumquats: wash kumquats and halve lengthwise. Place in a pan with the sugar and water. Bring to the boil and cook very slowly for 30 minutes. Serve warm over the cake.

For the glaze: melt all the ingredients in a double saucepan over barely simmering water until smooth. Pour over the cake while still warm.

Marquise Au Chocolat Blanc

To serve 10

1 tsp of powdered gelatine or 2 leaves of
  gelatine
350 ml (12 fl oz) double cream
275 g (10 oz) white chocolate in small pieces
50 ml (2 fl oz) water, plus 3 tbsp
25 ml (1 fl oz) liquid glucose
3 egg yolks
a thin genoise sponge, to cover top
pinch of salt

For the chocolate sauce
150 ml (¼ pint) water
100 g (4 oz) caster sugar
50 g (2 oz) cocoa powder

Soak the gelatine in 3 tbsp cold water.
Whip the cream and leave in a cool place.
Bring the 50 ml (2 fl oz) of water and
glucose to the boil, remove from the heat
and add the gelatine and chocolate. Stir
until the mixture is smooth. When the
mixture is blood temperature add the egg
yolks and fold in the cream. Place the
mixture in a 450 g (1 lb) loaf tin (no need to
grease it) and cover with the sponge, cut to
fit. Place in the refrigerator and leave for 24
hours.

To unmould: place the mould in very hot
water for a few seconds and then turn out.
Slice with a sharp knife heated in hot water
and dried. Place a slice on individual
serving plates and surround with some
chocolate sauce. To make the sauce, simply
dissolve the sugar in the water, bring to the
boil and whisk in the cocoa.

Chocolate Hazelnut Tuiles

To *make about* 20 *tuiles* 11 cm (4½ in) *diameter*

75 g (3 oz) hazelnuts
100 g (4 oz) caster sugar
50 g (2 oz) unsalted butter
pinch of salt
5 tsp cocoa powder
3 tbsp double cream
2 large egg whites
40 g (1½ oz) plain flour
2 tbsp rum
butter for greasing

Toast the nuts on a baking sheet in a preheated oven 180°C/350°F/mark 4 for 10 minutes. Rub them in a tea towel to remove the skins. Chop one third of the nuts and set aside. Finely grind the remaining nuts with the sugar in a blender or food processor. Preheat the oven to 220°C/425°F/mark 7. Cream the butter with a

wooden spoon, then blend in the sugar mixture, salt, cocoa and cream. Add the egg whites stirring only enough to blend. Sift, then fold in the flour and lastly the rum. Butter and flour a baking sheet. Lightly draw circles 11 cm (4½ in) in diameter about 5 cm (1½ in) apart. A bowl turned upside down and gently rotated can be used. Place 1 tbsp of the batter in the centre of each circle and spread it out with the back of the spoon to cover the circle. Sprinkle a pinch of the reserved nuts over the top. Bake for about 5 minutes, or until the edges are just beginning to darken. One at a time remove the tuiles with a spatula and place over a rolling pin, or in a cup, or shape around a metal or paper horn. Set the baking sheet on the open oven door to keep the tuiles warm and pliable. Work quickly as the tuiles crisp in a few seconds. Wait for oven to reach correct temperature before baking another batch. Store carefully in an airtight container.

Chocolate Soufflé Glacé

To serve 4

25 g (1 oz) cocoa powder
50 g (2 oz) plain chocolate in pieces
9 tbsp of water
100 g (3½ oz) sugar
2 egg whites
1–2 tbsp Grand Marnier or white rum
300 ml (½ pint) double cream, whipped

Prepare individual ramekins by wrapping a collar of greaseproof paper around each one to extend 3.75 cm (1½ in) above edge and tape in place. Melt the cocoa, chocolate and 4 tbsp of water together in a double saucepan set over hot but not boiling water. In a heavy pan dissolve the sugar with 5 tbsp water, bring to the boil and boil without stirring until the temperature reaches

115°C/239°F on a sugar thermometer. While the sugar is boiling whisk the egg whites until stiff. Pour the hot sugar syrup in a steady stream over the egg whites while continuing to whisk and keep whisking until the mixture is thick and cool. Using a metal spoon fold the chocolate into the whites, then fold in the whipped cream and flavouring. Spoon into the ramekins and freeze for at least 3 hours until firm. They can be frozen for 2 weeks if completely wrapped in foil. Remove paper collars and garnish with grated chocolate before serving. Remove from freezer and leave in refrigerator an hour or so before serving.

Chocolate Eclairs

To make about 12

For the choux pastry
Use the recipe Page 26

Crème patissière
500 ml (17 fl oz) milk
vanilla pod, split in two
6 egg yolks
100 g (4 oz) sugar
50 g (2 oz) flour

For the chocolate glaze
25 g (1 oz) cocoa powder
25 g (1 oz) caster sugar
5 tbsp water
150 g (6 oz) icing sugar

Prepare the choux pastry as in the recipe on page 26. Spoon into a pastry bag fitted with a 1 cm ($\frac{1}{2}$ in) plain nozzle. Grease a large baking sheet with butter. Pipe strips of dough 7 cm (3 in) long and well spaced apart. Cut off each length with a knife. Bake in a preheated oven 200°C/400°F/ mark 6 for 10 minutes. Reduce the oven to 190°C/375°F/mark 5 and bake a further 10 minutes. Pierce the ends of each shell, bake a further few minutes and then remove to a rack to cool.

To make the glaze: place cocoa, caster sugar and water in a small saucepan and bring to a boil stirring continuously. Take off the heat and sift in the icing sugar, stirring until blended. Dip the top of the éclairs into the glaze while it is still warm.

For the crème patissière: bring the milk and vanilla pod to a boil. Remove from the heat, cover, and leave for 15 minutes to infuse. Beat the egg yolks and sugar until thick and light, then stir in the sifted flour. Remove the pod from the milk (dry it and put with sugar for vanilla sugar) and bring back to a boil. Off the heat whisk in the egg mixture, return to a low heat and continue to whisk until the mixture thickens. Boil for at least 5 minutes to ensure flour loses its uncooked taste. Place a piece of cling-film over the surface to prevent a skin forming. Slice each éclair lengthwise and spoon the cream into the bottom half. Replace the tops and serve as soon as possible.

Chocolate Marquise

To serve 10

175 g (6 oz) plain chocolate
150 g (5 oz) butter, cut into small pieces
40 g (1½ oz) cocoa powder
2 eggs
75 g (3 oz) caster sugar
1–2 tbsp white rum (optional)
300 ml (½ pint) double cream, whipped
small cup of strong black coffee, unsweetened
sponge fingers

Line a 17 cm (6½ in) diameter charlotte mould with cling-film, leaving an overlap around the top edge to ease turning out. Melt the chocolate in the top of a double saucepan over hot but not boiling water. Whisk in the butter and then the cocoa and remove from the heat. Whisk the eggs and sugar over a bowl of hot water until the mixture is very thick and leaves a ribbon trail when the whisk is lifted. Using a metal spoon, fold in the chocolate mixture, rum, and then the whipped cream. Brush the sponge fingers with the cold coffee and line the bottom and sides of the mould, cutting them to shape where necessary. Spoon in the chocolate mixture, cover with cling film and refrigerate overnight. Turn out and leave at room temperature for an hour before serving. The marquise will keep for 3–4 days if refrigerated.

Chocolate Layered Cream Cake

To serve 8–10

100 g (4 oz) butter
50 g (2 oz) cocoa powder
2 eggs
225 g (8 oz) caster sugar
1 tsp vanilla extract
50 g (2 oz) self-raising flour
50 g (2 oz) plain flour
450 ml (¾ pint) double cream

For the chocolate curls
225 g (8 oz) plain chocolate
1 tbsp sunflower or groundnut oil

Grease a 20 cm (8 in) round cake tin and line the bottom with buttered greaseproof paper. Preheat the oven to 180°C/350°F/mark 4. Gently melt the butter in a small saucepan, stir in the cocoa until blended and set aside. In a medium-sized bowl, beat the eggs and caster sugar until light then add the cocoa mixture. Stir in the vanilla extract, then sift the flour over the mixture in small amounts, folding in with a metal spoon after each addition. Turn into the prepared tin and bake in the centre of the oven for 40–45 minutes. Leave in the tin for 10 minutes before turning out onto a cake rack. When the cake is completely cold wrap in cling-film and leave for 24 hours. This is not absolutely necessary, but makes slicing the cake easier. With a long, thin, sharp knife, using a sawing motion and working at eye level, slice the cake in half horizontally and then slice each half again making 4 discs. Use a spatula to help keep discs intact when you remove them. Whip the cream and sandwich between the layers and over the surface of the cake.

To make curls: stir the chocolate and oil in a double saucepan over hot, but not boiling, water until smooth. Pour onto a marble or other non-porous surface and spread out with a palette knife into a thin layer. Angle the blade of a straight knife and scrape across the chocolate to make curls for decorating top.

24

Profiteroles

To serve 6–8

For the choux pastry
100 g (3½ oz) flour
60 g (2½ oz) butter, cut into small pieces
175 ml (6 fl oz) water
½ tsp salt
2–3 eggs, size 2

For the chocolate sauce
75 ml (3 fl oz) water
25 g (1 oz) butter
150 g (5 oz) plain chocolate in small pieces
2 tbsp Grand Marnier

For the coffee cream filling
300 ml (½ pint) double cream
2 tbsp caster sugar
2 tsp instant coffee dissolved in 2 tbsp hot water

Sift the flour onto a square of greaseproof paper. Place the butter, water and salt in a saucepan and bring to the boil. Off the heat, using a wooden spoon, beat in all the flour at once. Continue to beat over a very low heat until the mixture is smooth and pulls away from the sides of the pan. Take off the heat and beat in the eggs one at a time, mixing in thoroughly before adding the next egg. Mix the third egg in a small bowl and add only enough to make a mixture that just falls from the spoon. Preheat the oven to 200° C/400° F/mark 6. Spoon the dough into a pastry bag fitted with a 1 cm (½ in) plain tube. Pipe mounds of dough far apart on a buttered baking sheet. Bake for 20 minutes, or until crisp and dry. Place on a rack and slice in two while still warm, to release the steam. If they are to be kept for more than a day place them in the hot oven, turned off and with the door open for 15 minutes to crisp further. Store in an airtight container when cool. Whip the cream with the other ingredients and spoon into the bottom halves of the shells.

For the sauce: bring water and butter to a boil, take off the heat and stir in the chocolate and liqueur. Sauce can be served hot or cold. Ice cream can replace the coffee cream and be served with the hot sauce.

Chocolate Chip Cookies

To make about 36

100 g (4 oz) butter
40 g (1½ oz) granulated sugar
75 g (3 oz) soft dark brown sugar
1 egg
1 tsp vanilla extract
100 g (4 oz) plain flour
2.5 ml (½ tsp) bicarbonate of soda
½ tsp salt
100 g (4 oz) bar of plain chocolate, cut into
  pea-sized pieces
50 g (2 oz) walnuts, chopped

Cream the butter and the two sugars together until light and fluffy. Lightly mix the egg and vanilla extract and gradually beat into the creamed mixture. Sift together the flour, bicarbonate of soda and salt and stir into the mixture. Finally stir in the chocolate pieces and the walnuts. Spoon heaped teaspoons of the mixture on to greased baking sheets, well spaced out. Bake in a preheated oven 180° C/350° F/ mark 4 for 10–15 minutes, or until lightly brown. Quickly remove the cookies with a spatula and place on any flat surface to cool. Store in an airtight container.

Chocolate Honey Ice Cream

To make 1.1 litres (2 pints)

900 ml (1½ pint) milk
110 ml (4 fl oz) acacia honey
150 ml (5 oz) caster sugar
6 egg yolks
50 g (2 oz) cocoa powder, sifted

In a heavy saucepan heat the milk, honey and half the sugar together until just below the boil. Remove from the heat and set aside. Whisk the egg yolks with the remaining sugar, pour over the hot milk while continuing to whisk, then return the mixture to the saucepan. Stir over a gentle heat until the mixture lightly coats a spoon. Remove from the heat and stir in the cocoa. Chill before freezing according to ice cream freezer instructions, or freeze to a slush, whisk and continue freezing until set.

Marble Pound Cake

To serve 8–10

75 g (3 oz) plain chocolate in pieces
250 g (9 oz) self-raising cake flour
250 g (9 oz) butter, room temperature
250 g (9 oz) caster sugar
4 large eggs, room temperature
1 tsp vanilla extract

Butter and flour a 1.1 litre (2 pint) tubular mould. Preheat oven to 180°C/350°F/mark 4. Sift the flour twice and set aside. Melt the chocolate in a double saucepan over hot but not boiling water and set aside.

Cream the butter, then beat in the sugar until light and fluffy. Mix the eggs with the vanilla and add it very gradually to the butter mixture. Using a metal spoon, fold the flour into the mixture a quarter at a time. Spoon half the mixture into the mould. Mix the melted chocolate into the remaining cake mixture and spoon into the mould. Plunge a knife into the batter and make several swirling movements to marblise. Bake for 1 hour, or until firm. Leave in the mould for 10 minutes before turning out onto a rack to cool. Store in an airtight container.

Petits Pots de Crême

(See illustration)

To serve 6

100 g (4 oz) plain chocolate in small pieces
450 ml (¾ pint) milk
1 tsp (level) instant coffee
4 egg yolks
1 tsp vanilla extract

Heat the chocolate, coffee and milk together over a very low heat, stirring, until the chocolate is completely dissolved. Off the heat beat in the egg yolks, one at a time and stir in the vanilla. Strain the mixture and pour into 6 mousse pots or ramekins. Place them in a baking dish filled with 2.5 cm (1 in) of hot water. Cover the mousse pots with foil or lids and bring to a simmer on top of the stove. Place in a preheated oven 170° C/325° F/mark 3, and bake for 35 minutes. Do not overcook them or allow the water to boil as this will alter their smooth consistency. Serve at room temperature. They will keep in a cool place for up to 24 hours.

Chocolate Crême Brulée

To serve 8

25 g (1 oz) cocoa powder
600 ml (1 pt) double cream
4 egg yolks
100 g (4 oz) caster sugar
1 tsp vanilla extract

Heat the cream, cocoa powder and 25 g (1 oz) of the sugar together until bubbles begin to form around the edge of the pan. Off the heat beat in the egg yolks, one at a time. Stir in the vanilla extract. Strain the mixture and pour into ramekins. Place in a baking pan and pour enough boiling water into the pan to come half-way up the sides of the ramekins. Bake in a preheated oven 180° C/350° F/mark 4 for 30 minutes. Cool, then refrigerate the ramekins for 4 hours or overnight. About 2 hours before serving, heat the grill until very hot. Sprinkle the remaining sugar over the ramekins to form a thin layer. Use more sugar if needed. Place the top of the ramekins about 8 cm (3 in) from the heat and grill for about 5 minutes until a golden crust forms. Watch them carefully to prevent the sugar burning.

Chocolate Roulade

To serve 8–10

175 g (6 oz) plain chocolate in small pieces
3 tbsp water
2 tbsp white rum or cognac
5 eggs
175 g (6 oz) caster sugar
icing sugar
300 ml (½ pint) whipping cream

Line a 33 × 24 cm (13½ × 9½ in) shallow tin with non-stick baking paper. Preheat oven to 180°C/350°F/mark 4. Melt the chocolate, water and liqueur together in the top of a double saucepan over hot but not boiling water. Separate the eggs, cracking the yolks into a large bowl and the whites into another bowl. Add the sugar to the yolks and whisk until pale in colour. Stir in the melted chocolate. Whisk the egg whites until stiff, then fold gently into the chocolate mixture, using a metal spoon. Pour into the prepared tin spreading evenly with a palette knife. Bake for 15 minutes. Remove from the heat, cover with a sheet of greaseproof paper and a damp cloth and leave overnight.

Turn the roulade out on to a sheet of greaseproof paper that has been well-dusted with icing sugar. Peel away the baking paper. Whip the cream and spread over the surface of the roulade. Roll up using the sugared paper to help. Chill for several hours. Before serving dust with icing sugar and cut into slices with a hot sharp knife.

Brownies

To make 16 squares

100 g (4 oz) butter
40 g (1½ oz) cocoa powder
2 eggs
225 g (8 oz) caster sugar
1 tsp vanilla extract
50 g (2 oz) self-raising flour
75 g (3 oz) chopped walnuts

Grease a 20 cm (8 in) square, shallow cake tin and line the bottom with greased greaseproof paper. Preheat the oven to 180°C/350°F/mark 4. Gently melt the butter in a small saucepan, stir in the cocoa until blended and set aside. In a medium-sized bowl, beat the eggs and caster sugar until light, then add the cocoa mixture. Stir in the vanilla extract, then sift in the flour and gently mix in. Add the nuts and turn in to the prepared tin. Bake in the centre of the oven for 30–35 minutes. Allow to cool completely in the tin before cutting into 2-in squares. The squares should be quite soft and moist inside.

Cream cheese brownies – a variation using full fat soft cheese

same ingredients as for basic recipe, plus:
25 g (1 oz) butter
100 g (4 oz) full fat soft cheese
75 g (3 oz) caster sugar
2 small eggs
1 tsp vanilla extract

Make up the brownie mixture following the basic recipe and pour into the tin.

Cream the butter with the cheese. Beat in the sugar and then the eggs, one at a time. Stir in the vanilla extract. Pour this cheese mixture over the chocolate and with the blade of a knife make several swirls to give a marbled effect. Bake in a preheated oven at 180°C/350°F/mark 4 for about 45 minutes. Allow to cool in the tin before cutting into squares.

Chocolate Eggs

To make about 6–7 eggs

6 small eggs
175 g (6 oz) praline, finely ground
275 g (10 oz) plain chocolate
175 ml (6 fl oz) double cream
4 tbsp white rum

Using a needle pierce a small hole in the pointed end of each egg. Use small scissors to enlarge the hole to a circle about 1 cm (½ in) in diameter. Shake the insides of the eggs out into a bowl and reserve for another use. Pour running water into the shells and shake until they are clean and empty. Dry in a low oven for 10 minutes.

Melt the chocolate carefully in a double saucepan filled with hot but not boiling water and stir until chocolate is smooth. Bring the cream to a boil in another saucepan and then stir into the melted chocolate. Stir in the praline and the rum. Spoon or pour the mixture into the eggs until full. Wash the shells and chill in the refrigerator until firm. Seal the holes with a small round label and place in an egg box with the labels at the bottom.

Mousse Suprême au Framboise

To serve 8

For the sponge roll
50 g (2 oz) self-raising flour
25 g (1 oz) cocoa powder
3 eggs
100 g (3½ oz) caster sugar
1 tsp vanilla extract

For the mousse
1 tsp gelatine
3 tbsp cold water
2 tbsp raspberry liqueur (optional)
225 g (8 oz) plain chocolate
3 tbsp milk
15 g (½ oz) butter
4 eggs
pinch of salt

For the final assembly
3 tbsp raspberry jam dissolved in 3 tbsp water
crême anglaise (see recipe page 48)

Chocolate sauce, for marbling
50 g (2 oz) plain chocolate
15 g (½ oz) butter
4 tbsp milk
150 g (¼ lb) fresh raspberries for garnish

Line a 30 × 24 cm (12½ × 9½ in) Swiss roll tin with non-stick baking parchment. Preheat oven to 200°C/400°F/mark 6. Sift the flour and cocoa powder together three times and set aside. Whisk the eggs and sugar together in a bowl set over a pan of hot water. Whisk until mixture is very thick and leaves a ribbon trail when the whisk is lifted. Using a metal spoon fold the cocoa and flour into the mixture by quarters. Pour into the tin and spread level. Bake for 8—10 minutes. Remove from the oven, loosen the sides with a knife and turn over on to a clean cloth, lightly sprinkled with caster sugar. Peel away the paper and roll from the narrower edge with the cloth into a cylinder. Set aside until needed.

To make the mousse: mix the gelatine with the water and liqueur and leave to soften. Place over gentle heat and stir until gelatine is dissolved. Meanwhile melt the chocolate, milk and butter in a double saucepan over barely simmering water. Crack each of the eggs, putting the whites in a bowl (preferably copper) and dropping the yolks, one at a time, into the chocolate mixture; stir in the gelatine. Whisk the egg whites with the salt until stiff. Using a metal spoon fold the whites into the chocolate.

To assemble: use a 1.4 litre (2½ pint) capacity loaf tin. Melt the raspberry jam with the water, unroll the cake and brush the raspberry syrup over the top. Line the loaf tin with cling-film, then press in the cake leaving a flap at the top to make a lid. Fill the centre with the mousse, fold the cake over the top and refrigerate for at least 6 hours. The chocolate sauce is made by gently melting the ingredients together.

Chocolate Chestnut Mousse Cake

To serve 10

100 g (4 oz) plain chocolate
4 eggs, separated
200 g (7 oz) sugar
225 g (8 oz) canned unsweetened chestnut
  purée
pinch of salt
1 tsp vanilla extract
150 ml (¼ pint) whipping cream
cocoa powder
crème anglaise (see page 48 for recipe)

Line a 30 × 24 cm (12½ × 9½ in) Swiss roll tin with non-stick baking parchment. Preheat oven to 180°C/350°F/mark 4. Melt the chocolate in the top of a double saucepan over hot, but not boiling water. Beat the egg yolks with three-quarters of the sugar, then beat in the chestnut purée, vanilla, and melted chocolate. Sieve the mixture into a clean bowl. Whip the egg whites and salt until stiff, add the remaining sugar and whisk until glossy. Using a metal spoon fold a quarter of the egg whites into the chestnut mixture. Carefully fold in the rest of the whites and spread over the prepared tin. Bake for 15–20 minutes. Leave in the tin to cool. The cake can be prepared to this stage 24 hours ahead of time. An hour before serving, whip the cream, cut the cake into 3 equal strips and sandwich with the cream. Sieve a layer of cocoa over the top and serve with crème anglaise.

Chocolate Cinnamon Soufflé

To serve 4

1.25 litre (2 pint) or 4 × 300 ml (½ pint)
capacity soufflé dishes
butter for greasing
1 tsp ground cinnamon
5 tbsp caster sugar
125 g (5 oz) plain chocolate in small pieces
150 ml (¼ pint) double cream
1 tsp instant coffee dissolved in 2 tbsp hot
water
3 egg yolks
5 egg whites
crème anglaise (see page 48 for recipe)

Preheat oven to 220°C/425°F/mark 6.
Mix the cinnamon and caster sugar
together. Grease the soufflé dishes and
sprinkle the insides with 2 tbsp of the
cinnamon mixture. Shake out any excess.
Heat the chocolate and cream over very low
heat stirring until smooth. Remove from
the heat and beat in the egg yolks and the
coffee. Whisk the egg whites until stiff,
then whisk in the cinnamon sugar until
mixture is glossy. Gently heat the chocolate
mixture until just hot to the touch. Using a
metal spoon fold a quarter of the whites into
the chocolate. Add this mixture to the
remaining egg whites and carefully fold all
together. Bake the small soufflés for 7–9
minutes. Allow 12–14 for the large one.
Serve immediately accompanied by crème
anglaise.

The chocolate egg yolk mixture can be
prepared several hours ahead. Reheat until
it is just hot before whisking and folding in
the egg whites.

Crême Anglaise

600 ml (1 pint) milk
vanilla pod, split in two
5 egg yolks
75 g (3 oz) caster sugar

Bring the milk with the vanilla pod to a boil in a heavy saucepan. Remove from the heat and cover. Whisk the yolks and sugar until thick and pale. Remove the vanilla pod from the milk and pour the milk over the egg yolks, whisking continuously. Pour the mixture back into the saucepan, set over low heat and cook stirring continuously with a wooden spatula until the mixture just coats the spatula. Do not allow the mixture to boil. Sieve the mixture and allow to cool, stirring occasionally.

Aunt Lillie
    From Gladys
I remember your coffee Cake 'Lovely'